GETTYSBURG

This Hallowed Ground

Poetry by Kent Gramm

Photographs by Chris Heisey

TIDE-MARK PRESS

Windsor, Connecticut

© 2003 by Chris Heisey, Kent Gramm, and Tide-mark Press

Published by Tide-mark Press, Ltd.
P.O. Box 20, Windsor, CT 06095-0020

Printed and bound in Korea by Samhwa Printing Co.
Book design by Dan Veale

Library of Congress Cataloging-in-Publication Data

Gramm, Kent and Heisey, Chris
Gettysburg: This Hallowed Ground
144 p. cm.

ISBN 1-55949-884-6 Hardcover Edition

Library of Congress Control Number
2003113659

CONTENTS

We are Met on a Great Battlefield

By Chris Heisey

༺✿༻

O n July 4, 1863, the heavens began to pour upon the meadows and rocky ridges surrounding Gettysburg as a series of violent thunderstorms pummelled the small Pennsylvania town. The rain lasted for days, leading many to surmise that the torrents were God's tears of sadness, and that the thunder was his rage.

I made my first trip to Gettysburg when I was an eight-year-old boy; it was also raining that June day in 1972. I lived only an hour north of the hallowed battlefield, so I thought the trip was no great journey. Yet sloshing about the battlefield with my parents as Tropical Storm Agnes deluged the killing fields was intensely memorable. I remember feeling a sense of awe, and it hasn't left me since. Some 30 years later, the sheer magnitude of the carnage continues to strike me with wonder. I grew up in a town with a population of 25,000 bordered by a rival town with the same demographics. The horrific bloodletting is staggering to imagine — more than 50,000 soldiers, blue and gray, fell as battlefield casualties during the three-day battle of Gettysburg on July 1–3, 1863. Every one of my neighbors would have been killed, wounded or captured.

Despite the immensity of death, Gettysburg is a place blessed with monumental beauty. The historic landscape rolls with emotion and speaks to you if you take the time to listen. Dotting the sacred battleground are some 1,400 monuments that serve as testaments to the sacrifice so freely given that July long ago. Gettysburg is the home of the world's largest outdoor sculpture display, and, like no other place in the world, this place stirs the soul.

Upon returning a few years after the battle, one veteran who had faced death remarked while looking out on the battlefield, "This is holy ground." Amen.

The same year that I made my inaugural pilgrimage to Gettysburg, I had an engaging second-grade teacher who whetted my mind for learning about history. There at Palmyra's Pine Street Elementary School — a place that still stands now as it did then — Mrs. Sohlman encouraged me to read and write. I vividly remember thinking about the Civil War there in my small classroom, sitting next to my best friend as a gentle February snow innocently blanketed the playground just outside the windows. On the bulletin boards across the room hung two boldly colored pictures of Washington and Lincoln. Early on, Lincoln became my hero because of his perfect imperfectness. Never in my mind has there ever been a better writer than Lincoln.

Lincoln came to Gettysburg some four months after the battle in the browns of November to dedicate the cemetery where thousands were buried — many with the marker "Unknown U.S. Soldier." It seems such a pity to die without one's name or identity. The very thought scared Lincoln.

"We are met on a great battlefield," Lincoln tells us in his famous address delivered there in the National Cemetery. When I first heard those words at Pine Street Elementary, I wondered to myself what those words really meant. What was President Lincoln telling me, the little boy?

Oftentimes growing up, I strayed from learning more about the Civil War, but the war was always close to my heart. One year on my birthday, a kind neighbor gave me *The Golden Book of the Civil War,* which sparked my interest in learning. The book's colorful maps and striking artwork dazzled my eye and touched my heart. Hundreds of times, I have leafed through that dusty book. My love of books began with this simple but profound book. Today, the book's binding is duct-taped together, and it has that distinct smell that only a heavily used book has. My son now pages through that book just as I did. Books matter.

When I was a teen, I played sports and dreaded doing homework. But when something related to the Civil War came on television, I paid attention. Off to college I went with hardly a clue as to what the will of my life was to be. I wrote only one term paper in college, and it was entitled "Slavery: The Cause of the Civil War." I wasn't an "A" student by any stretch, but I earned one for that paper because I researched and wrote from my heart. I have never forgotten that valuable lesson.

I graduated in 1986 still searching for my place in this world. Days after graduation, my mother bought me a 35mm SLR camera from Sears and for us that was a big expense. That camera, however simple, taught me how to see rather than just look. Saint Matthew aptly tells us in his Gospel, "The eye is the lamp of the body. So if your eye is healthy, your whole body will be full of light." Seeking good light has always been my keenest desire as an image taker.

In 1990, on a number of chilly September nights, I watched Ken Burns' PBS Civil War documentary. I was enthralled by the visual presentation and if there has ever been a finer use of television, I have not seen it. I especially appreciated the dramatic cinematography that caught the battlefields in such telling and evocative light. Union Colonel Joshua Chamberlain of the 20th Maine had it right when he said, "In great deeds something abides. On great fields something stays…. Men and women from generations that know not, heart-drawn to see where and by whom great things were suffered and done for them, shall come to this deathless field to ponder and dream. On a great battlefield something still abides."

With that in mind's eye, I set out at 4:00 a.m. a few days after watching the Burns series, making the hour's drive to Gettysburg. Getting up early was a small sacrifice, as I was conditioned young in life to awake early by a father who was and still is a milkman. In the joy of summer, I would travel with him and enjoy the majesty of the rising sun and the new dawn those rays serenely brought forth.

When I arrived on the battlefield, the air was delicately crisp as the sun began to brighten the eastern sky. I was amazed as the hues of the sky changed with every moment. My camera was loaded with Kodachrome 25, and as I tripped the shutter silhouetting an artillery piece against the auburn sky, my heart pounded in my chest. "Every child is an artist," Picasso once said, adding, "the problem is how to remain an artist once one grows up."

I few days later, I reviewed my slides the old-fashioned way by holding them up to a window. "Wow!" was my first impression and, though my composition was suspect and my angle of view weak, I knew a passion was beginning. And since, I have returned to Gettysburg time after time with my camera loaded ready to freeze a moment in time. I have visited Gettysburg more than 1,200 times. Once the thermometer had plummeted to negative 23 degrees; and six months later, I walked the battlefield with my tripod slung over my shoulder in 104-degree heat. Blizzards have raged and tornados have marched across the open plains just as the Confederates did 140 years ago. In autumn, the leaves go ablaze and the crimson colors stand out when fog envelops the monuments. But my favorite time at Gettysburg is winter, maybe because I am a northerner. Snow and ice clinging to the soldiers made of granite and bronze are among my most beloved moments to capture. The monuments stand for real soldiers who were once here, lest we forget.

Perhaps my most magical moment at Gettysburg occurred on January 1, 2000. That dawn of the new millennium was briefly spectacular as the winter's low sun angle cast a shadow on the Brian Barn that only lasted a minute before the clouds swallowed up the light. Not for another thousand years will light under those circumstances fall upon Gettysburg. I was blessed for that moment, and as an artist-photographer, nothing humbles me more than good light, no matter how brief, given from above.

Collaborating on a book with Kent Gramm is a dream come true. As a lover of books, I have always wanted to contribute to the vast quantity of Civil War books. It seems as though for every day since the war ended in April 1865, at least one book has been published about the war. Why another? Why not? More can and should be said about this war. When I fearfully approached Dr. Gramm at a seminar that he was hosting at Gettysburg in 2002, I did so because I knew of no other writer who expressed in words what I have tried to express with my imagery. In 1994, I read his book *Gettysburg: A Meditation on War and Values*—not only did the book inspire me to put feeling to film even more, it helped me make sense of the immense tragedy that Gettysburg and the Civil War are really about. "The frantic nature of our occupations and amusements show that we don't believe in what we are doing," Dr. Gramm writes in the conclusion. This book is a colossal call to think. It's a siren to those who only seek knowledge and forget to pray for wisdom. In my eye, no writer today puts Civil War verse to paper better than Dr. Gramm.

I will continue to return to Gettysburg and the scores of other Civil War battlefields where the image well will never dry up. Something abides. The sacred mysteries that flit about the battlefield come in the form of light. "And God said, 'Let there be light.' And God saw that the light was good," the first chapter of the Bible states. Mine eyes have seen the glory of good light at Gettysburg. I am thankful to Him.

"No matter how slow the film, Spirit always stands still long enough for the photographer It has chosen," a legendary photographer wrote a few years ago. Whether one walks the fields at the Rose Farm or spends time musing in the National Cemetery, Spirit does stand still here as in no other place. More than 50,000 soldiers bled here and only some were able to return to remember their baptism of blood. "Gettysburg has become the place of all places. This is one of the great battlefields of the world. There is no place on the broad earth…where so much has been done by art and labor to make it worthy of pilgrimage here," a Union soldier wrote on his first visit back to Pennsylvania after the war.

Nearly 2 million people visit Gettysburg each year, yet ironically on a frigid, snowy day, finding one visitor is a challenge. That's the beauty of Gettysburg. One cold, blustery night a few years ago, I stood on Little Round Top as the sun's last rays touched Gettysburg. I was alone with just my musings, or so I thought. Done pondering, and a bit frozen in time, I began walking ahead to modernity and my car. Faintly I heard the sound of a bugle, playing my favorite call, *Taps*. The tears welled up in my eyes as I approached the lone bugler perfectly dressed in kepi and cloak. In the darkness, I couldn't tell whose side he was on, but I could see that he also had tears in his eyes. I nodded in acknowledgement as I cried on and he played on. It was then that I knew what Lincoln meant when he said, "We are Met on a Great Battlefield" to that little boy who grew up a little north of the beautiful battlefield of Gettysburg.

Chris E. Heisey
December 2003
Mechanicsburg, Pennsylvania

"A thing of beauty is a joy for ever"

– Keats

❧✦✤✦❧

Why visit a Civil War battlefield—or revisit it through photographs? Some people see such places as large cemeteries or reminders of our inhumanity. True as those impressions are, they are only partial truths. The larger truth is that these visits and photographs do us good. The very fact that the battle has passed and once again the meadows bloom and the fields produce grain reminds us that there are larger truths than war, and that we have reason to hope. A transformation has taken place at Gettysburg—a transformation each of us may hope for in our own lives. Time spent at Gettysburg gives us intimations of eternity.

The photographs of Chris Heisey remind one that truth and facts are not synonymous, that history has meaning that goes beyond written documentation. We have placed some lines of poetry with each image because the photographs are pieces of art, and as such they convey some essential things about the meaning of the battlefield.

> *Nor do we merely feel these essences*
> *For one short hour; no, even as the trees*
> *That whisper round a temple become soon*
> *Dear as the temple's self, so does the moon,*
> *The passion poesy, glories infinite,*
> *Haunt us till they become a cheering light*
> *Unto our souls, and bound to us so fast,*
> *That, whether there be shine, or gloom o'ercast,*
> *They always must be with us, or we die.*
> — Keats, *Endymion I, 25 – 33*

Of course, many who look at this book will say, "It would be better with only the photographs." They may well be right. You do not need lines of writing to tell you what to think or feel about these photographs, and the photographs are more beautiful than my words can express. Think of the lines as footnotes—or as attempts by one person to translate into words the beauty of these fields. At best they can help some of us move our feelings into thoughts, and thoughts into the imagination.

In any case, the words are forgettable but the images impress themselves upon us. On the fields at Gettysburg, and seeing these photographs, a person perceives a kind of sanctity—a sanctity that is truth. The poems express a skepticism of many things, but they all reiterate what John Keats wrote in a letter dated November 22, 1817:

> *I am certain of nothing but of the holiness of the Heart's affections*
> *and the truth of the Imagination—What the imagination seizes as*
> *Beauty must be truth—whether it existed before or not.*

The photographer does not only record the beauty and truth of a scene; the photographer creates an image. Artistic photography such as that of Chris Heisey makes something new. As Keats went on to say, "… our Passions … in their sublime [are] creative of essential beauty." Anyone who has visited Gettysburg more than 1,200 times, as Chris Heisey has, certainly works with passion—a passion that the beauty of the fields at Gettysburg makes sublime.

But are these pictures in any sense truth? Can the mayhem and cruelty that are war be made into something both beautiful and honest? And can the terrors and ugliness that plague today's world be redeemed by visits to a beautiful landscape frozen in timelessness? Again, the letter of John Keats:

> *The Imagination may be compared to Adam's dream —*
> *he awoke and found it truth.*

The beauty of these images is an intimation of a newer world, one in which, despite what we have done and suffered in this world, we "under God, shall have a new birth of freedom" — for our hearts, our minds, and our spirits. As long as we respond to beauty, there is hope.

The words alongside these photographs are responses to beauty. The tyranny of our day-to-day lives tells us that beauty is only a luxury, mere decoration. But everything else about us tells us that beauty is a necessity: a baby chuckles at colors and shadows, a child sings rhymes, and nearly everyone likes some form of music. The Grand Canyon and the Rocky Mountains receive millions of visitors yearly — and they go there for beauty. So too Gettysburg: visitors come with curiosity, but leave with a deep and terrible beauty engraved upon their imaginations. The best way to understand something is to see it by the light of beauty. The battlefield at Gettysburg is like the strange and beautiful Grecian urn:

> *When old age shall this generation waste,*
> *Thou shalt remain, in midst of other woe*
> *Than ours, a friend to man, to whom thous say'st,*
> *"Beauty is truth, truth beauty, — that is all*
> *Ye know on earth, and all ye need to know."*

Kent Gramm
December 2003
Lake Geneva, Wisconsin

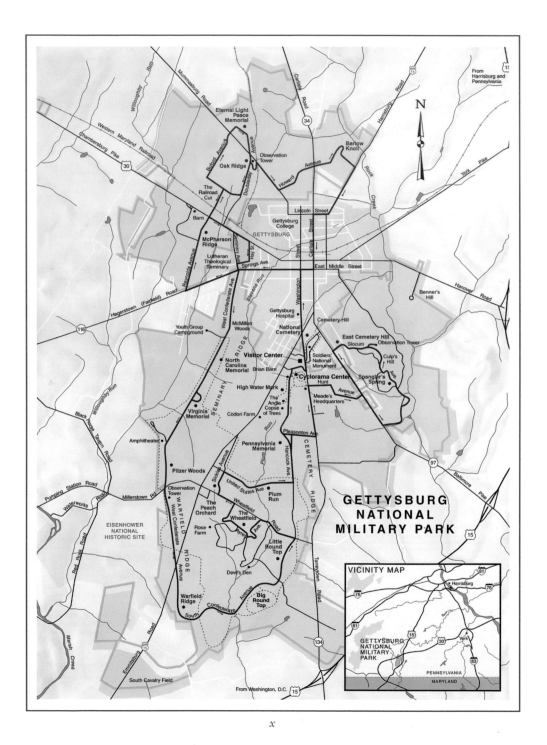

THE BATTLE OF GETTYSBURG

Eleven slaveholding states declared themselved independent of the United States following the 1860 presidential election in which Abraham Lincoln, an antislavery candidate, was elected. These Southern states formed a Confederacy and prepared to defend their territory against Federal volunteers mobilized by President Lincoln to enforce the laws of the United States.

For two years, United States armies operating in the Mississippi River basin, primarily under General Ulysses S. Grant, steadily reclaimed large areas of the Southern Confederacy. In the Eastern theater between Washington, D.C. and the Confederate capital of Richmond, Virginia, Federal forces lost a series of battles to the brilliant and audacious General Robert E. Lee and his Army of Northern Virginia. None of these eastern battles was decisive, however; none caused the United States government or the Northern people to give up the war for the Union. Therefore, General Lee decided to march his army across the Potomac River, the de facto boundary between the loyal and rebellious states, to try to win a victory in Pennsylvania, which might open the U.S. capital and government to capture, resulting in official recognition of the Confederate States of America and an end to the war. Resounding defeat or complete destruction of the Union's chief army in the east, the Army of the Potomac, was the primary element of Confederate hopes.

In June of 1863, the Army of Northern Virginia moved north using a route through the Shenandoah Valley, concealed behind the Blue Ridge mountains. The Army of the Potomac broke camp at Fredericksburg, Virginia, and raced north on the east side of the mountains, staying between Lee's army and Washington. At the end of June, President Lincoln dismissed the last in a line of incompetent commanding generals, placing the aggressive and modest George Gordon Meade in command of the Army of the Potomac.

Lee had sent his three corps of infantry and one of cavalry into Pennsylvania separately to increase their efficiency in seizing horses, supplies, and former slaves. By the end of June, Ewell's Second Corps was at York and Harrisburg, Hill's Second Corps was at Cashtown just west of Gettysburg, and Longstreet's First Corps was near Chambersburg behind Hill's Corps.

Meade's army consisted of seven infantry corps, each approximately half the size of its Confederate counterpart, plus one cavalry corps. Both armies possessed several hundred pieces of artillery, bringing Lee's army to roughly 80,000 men and Meade's to roughly 90,000. Not knowing the Confederates' exact wherabouts, Meade kept his corps spread across northern Maryland, with cavalry and his First Corps of infantry advancing across the Pennsylvania line into Gettysburg, where roads from York, Harrisburg, and Chambersburg met roads coming up from Maryland. On June 30, Buford's Union cavalry encountered advancing Confederate troops just west of Gettysburg. The Rebel infantry withdrew, but Union cavalry quickly discovered Ewell's Corps to be moving toward Gettysburg from the north, and Hill's and Longstreet's from the west.

Meade ordered all corps of the Army of the Potomac to march toward Gettysburg. On the morning of July 1, two of Hill's three infantry divisions (15,000 men) advanced on Gettysburg down the Chambersburg/Cashtown road. They were met by Buford's 2,800 Union soldiers, who fought dismounted in line of battle and forced the first division in Hill's column (Heth's) to leave the road and deploy into line of battle, which consumed considerable time. Heth's Division then attacked, and the Yankee cavalry slowly gave way, moving back toward Gettysburg. When the cavalry reached McPherson's Ridge, they withdrew as freshly arrived infantry of Reynolds's First Corps hurried into line. The Iron Brigade (First Brigade, First Division, First Corps) counterattacked through McPherson's Woods and across a shallow stream called Willoughby Run, capturing upwards of 200 men from Archer's Brigade, along with General Archer himself. One regiment of the Iron Brigade, reinforced by two New York regiments, attacked three regiments of a Mississippi brigade positioned in a railroad cut, capturing another 200–300 men. Heth withdrew his division.

During the early afternoon, Pender's Division of Hill's Corps moved into position with some of Heth's battered division on a mile-wide front overlapping the southern end of the Union First Corps' line, which ran North-South, facing west, along McPherson's Ridge. The northern flank of the blue line was threatened by Ewell's Corps, just arriving on the field from the north. The First Corps' line was extended perpendicularly, west-east, by the newly arrived Eleventh Corps, which was forced to deploy across low, flat ground north of town. At about 3:00 p.m., the Confederate attacks opened along an arc several miles long, converging on the shorter Union lines joined at a right angle. Outnumbered and outflanked, the Union First Corps was forced back to Seminary Ridge after some of the most intense fighting of the war. To the north, Rodes's division of Ewell's Corps was at first repulsed with heavy loss, but before long, Ewell's three divisions attacked the Eleventh Corps and the northern flank of the First Corps. After stubborn resistance by some of its units, the Eleventh Corps fled south through town. Making a stand at the Lutheran Theological Seminary and northward, the remnants of the First Corps eventually had its left flank turned, just as Ewell's Corps moved down behind them in pursuit of the Eleventh Corps. The Iron Brigade lost over 60 percent of its men defending McPherson's Woods and the Seminary grounds. Of the 20 regiments in the Army of the Potomac's seven infantry corps, which suffered the heaviest percentages of loss at Gettysburg, 16 regiments were from the First Corps and four from the Eleventh; the five brigades with heaviest losses were all from the First

Corps. Confederate numbers of killed and wounded were even higher, with some North Carolina regiments displaying appalling bravery in attacking Union infantry and artillery just north of the Seminary.

The First and Eleventh Corps streamed back through the streets of Gettysburg, pursued ineffectively by Confederate units exhausted and decimated by the morning and afternoon fighting. Union survivors formed a defensive line on Cemetery Hill at the south end of town. Sacrificing 50 percent of its men, the First Corps had bought time for the Army of the Potomac. Other infantry corps arrived through the evening and night, and by morning the Union line extended three miles north-south in the shape of an inverted fishhook, the barb up at the northeast on Culp's Hill, the bend across Cemetery Hill, its spine running down along Cemetery Ridge, and the eye resting on a half-cleared hill called Little Round Top. Lee's army stretched along an arc that eventually extended six miles, the intent being to attack both Union flanks and crush the Army of the Potomac towards the middle.

Confederate plans for July 2nd called for a diversionary attack by Ewell's Corps on the Union left on Culp's Hill, while Longstreet's and Hill's Corps launched the major offensive against the Union left, which careless Confederate reconnaisance assumed to terminate short of Little Round Top. As two divisions of Longstreet's corps marched a roundabout route toward the Union left, General Dan Sickles disregarded General Meade's instructions and moved his Third Corps forward off the Cemetery Ridge line to occupy high ground along the Emmitsburg Road in front of the Army of the Potomac's position. Sickles placed one division along the road and another on a line angling back from the road. The second division ran through a peach orchard, behind the Rose Farm, through a wheatfield, across a small ridge, and terminated in a jumble of enormous rocks called Devil's Den. Behind Sickles's left, Round Top lay vacant, as troops previously covering it had been transferred to Culp's Hill in anticipation of the Third Corps occupying it. Sickles's rash and insubordinate move confused the Confederate high command and delayed Longstreet's offensive. However, when McLaws (of Longstreet's Corps) emerged from his circuitous march, he found not an unoccupied Emmitsburg Road with a half mile of open ground behind it, but rather two divisions of Federal infantry supported by artillery. Longstreet adjusted by ordering Hood's division to march past McLaws and attack from farther south.

Union General G. K. Warren, realizing that Little Round Top was undefended and about to be attacked, sent appeals for troops. Colonel Strong Vincent, acting on his own responsibility, moved his brigade to the hill just in time to receive a series of attacks by Evander Law's Alabama Brigade. The far left of Vincent's line, held by the 20th Maine, resisted the 15th Alabama's repeated uphill charges that threatened to turn the Union left flank. The two regiments closed to hand-to-hand fighting, but here and all along its line, Vincent's Brigade held, receiving reinforcements and secured the southerly anchor of the Union line.

Texans and Alabamians had meanwhile overrun Devil's Den and its rocky ridge just as Georgians and South Carolinians attacked the Wheatfield. Third Corps troops, stretched too thinly, resisted desperately as determined Southern brigades broke Sickles's entire line. Union reinforcements from the Second and Fifth Corps vigorously counterattacked. In the space of an hour, 3,000 men were killed and wounded in the small Wheatfield alone. By evening, though Lee's men had crashed through all of the Third Corps positions and part of one brigade had actually advanced all the way to Cemetery Ridge, the Army of the Potomac had been repelled and thrown back all Confederate troops except those in and around Devil's Den.

Heavy fighting then flared up to the north. A Confederate assault on Cemetery Hill was driven away, but only after some attackers had achieved a temporary lodgement amid Union artillery. As night fell, Rebels attacked Union lines on Culp's Hill, capturing a small section of the Federal trenches, but being repulsed along the rest of the line.

Union troops counterattacked at dawn, establishing firm defenses on Culp's Hill that resisted several hours of Confederate attacks. Later in the morning, Union cavalry scuffled with Stuart's troopers several miles east of the main battlefield, resulting in a tactical draw that prevented Stuart from bringing his cavalry into the Union rear, where its supplies, ammunition, and reserve artillery were parked. Meanwhile, Confederate officers meticulously planned a daring and carefully conceived assault on the Union center on upper Cemetery Ridge.

At 1:00 p.m., Confederate artillery opened the greatest barrage ever fired in North America; the sound was heard as far away as Pittsburgh, across the mountains over 200 miles away. Federal artillery, superior in command, munitions, and experience, responded. Though the Southerners received more damage than they inflicted during the 1-2 hour barrage, they partially achieved their goals of reducing the number of Federal guns at the attack's objective point and depleting Federal long-range ammunition.

Then Confederate infantry went forward: two and one-half divisions, approximately 13,000 men, in what became known as Pickett's Charge, named for the Virginia general who exercised immediate field command during the attack. Avoiding high and open ground, Confederate troops had positioned themselves in two wings. One lay behind a low ridgeline directly across from the objective point of the attack, a clump of trees three-quarters of a mile across open fields; Pickett's own division had moved much closer to Union lines, though farther south, concealing themselves along a depression near the Emmitsburg Road. Braving artillery fire and eventually small-arms fire, the attacking Confederates advanced for 20 minutes across the fields, executing the diagonal and left-flank maneuvers necessary to join their two wings with a precision that inspired Union defenders with awe, pity, and horror. Confederate courage was surpassed only by the thin blue line that awaited the attackers, most notably the 69th Pennsylvania, whose 300 men faced a dense mass of several thousand Rebels coming directly at them. Union defenders did not merely await the shock of impact, however; Union Second Corps units moved out to attack both flanks of the Southern advance, and two brigades charged the Confederates who broke through on a narrow front near the Copse of Trees. Pickett's Charge was destroyed, with fewer than half the attackers returning to Confederate lines.

The Battle of Gettysburg resulted in 50,000 soldiers killed, wounded, and captured, 28,000 of whom were Confederate. The battle was the turning point of the Civil War in the East in at least two respects: First, the soldiers of the Army of the Potomac knew that their efforts, not merely Southern mistakes, had won the greatest battle ever fought in America, and they gained the confidence and assurance that saw the war through to the end; the Army of Northern Virginia lost one-third of its veteran soldiers, and Lee was never again able to mount offensives as he had done prior to and at Gettysburg. Second, and of even greater significance, the battle became the occasion of Abraham Lincoln's Gettysburg Address, which gave meaning to the tragedy of the Civil War as a struggle to win for the "nation, under God, a new birth of freedom" and assure that "government of the people, by the people, for the people, shall not perish from the earth."

BLUE AND GRAY

A fence begins in nowhere, ends in nowhere,
coursing through a strawy field at dawn:
a tense transparency suspends the air —
a photographer's flat box presses it all
odorless, the humus and adze-hewn wood
visual, translated, rectangular
and not the faintest lingering taste of blood.
Instead, chemicals have siphoned from these
an image — light from light — the unknown left
unknown and darkening into distance, dark blue —
or dark gray? Dark gray like the fence itself,
which is as much dark blue as gray — and you
see nothing in the sky at this old hour,
but on the ground the ancient solitude of flowers.

The man of stone before,
no background shapes or figures we must sift
and simplify to understand this war …

... a symmetry of pattern and design
put there by nature and the shooter's eye.

*W*here Krishna pointed, there did doomed Arjuna go,
for duty is the only will of God we know.

. . . batteries of chance spring to flame
across the lovely lawns of finitude.

You mortals craning necks down there below,
if but this stone could make you understand:
  it is more painful than you'll ever know
to wear your doubt and faith. I was a man.

Look away, look away, if you ever
loved a soldier . . .

A three-inch rifle's tube is beautiful,
its shape a graceful liquifaction . . .

*In this little valley where a run
not unlike Jordan generates a mist,
the cannon situates itself, an urn
aimed sideways down the hollow through a steam
of breathing, its wheels at rest endlessly
repeating what was, is now, and shall be.*

. . . no calm explanations need be taught
to the stumbling usher of the mind:
at once the blank, bold, silver screen of time
is rolled and thrown with all that God hath wrought.

A coal black cannon in a shadow, hollow,
aimed at some face; only the cut iron plate
of light, a bronze null ending the barrel,
shines: ready, it only stands and awaits
that fine, final word — that righteous command
as natural as dawn, urgent, patient,
unmoved as guns at the sight of dead men —
one winged light, a world-renouncing roar,
eternity in silence, love in war.

And summer comes again to Gettysburg,
leafing as if nothing ever dies —
though is it hot today, and no leaf stirs.
The thinker bows his head and wonders why —
the soldier does the things that never were
and asks impossibles of earth and sky.

Scattered knapsacks, rifles, lay all about;
a score of horses squealing in their blood,
another score stretched coldly in the mud:
a scene of confused defense and of rout.

. . . again the angry men, again their blood,
again the curses and the screams of pain;
the bullets sought the dull and sickening thud,
and rifle smoke made dim the light above
the trees: that coronet obscure again —
the cool, eternal, distant crown of love.

. . . many years ago
a man named Abraham once brought his son
to sacrifice him on a slippery stone —
his own beloved son, his only one —
obeying to the letter God's hard word.
And then as Abraham lifted the knife —
his trembling son stares deep into his face —
the voice returns and spares young Isaac's life.
And from that child has sprung our careful race,
as quick as ever to obey the Lord
but never trusting anything to love.
Joyless Abraham now lies beneath the sod,
a sacrifice to Him who broods above
sick and tired of being worshiped like a god.

COURAGE

These Carolinians were cast in bronze
by the same hand that chiseled Mount Rushmore.
They wave their blunt muskets at The Faces:
Washington, Jefferson, and the man's hand
points brave murder at Abraham Lincoln . . .

The next mute, inglorious Milton should
consider what courage and valor cost
in paradises divided and lost.

MR. LINCOLN

The iron arms that clove rails are severed
from the monumentally die-cast bust;
he only broods now, like the Holy Ghost —
handless, speechless, harmlessly revered.
What does he think of us? We think we know,
but penetrating looks are only looks.
What if? What if? — a game for holy books
dreamily pure as angels in the snow.

In prayer, imagination shapes the awe
our lives rough-hew, a work of tired arms
against the wildness of a moral law
that yields its mysteries as rebels yield —
howling rows of honorable, lethal forms
struck down and silent in a sunny field.

TRANSFIGURATION

One day the war will disappear, as all
wars do; the trace along the worming rails
will waver into story like flaked nails
from the True Cross, this rough cut wood fallen
into soft mold. One day the ignorant
will graze on pavement here, where once the guns
of civil war poured horror through the sons
of Jesus in the names of Lee and Grant.
And Davis—all the predatory names
of fate: scraped of clay they will have risen
from this grass to a firmament one day—
the unknown men deposed in molding graves—
the mortal, reading face of Mr. Lincoln
cast into the sun's unfailing rays.

GLORY

And if the muskets guess the subtle tides
of men, and catch them at unlucky ebbs;
and if the glaring noons of sooty blood
can light to Hades the new, wandering dead;
and if the causes men fight aching for
can reach into their very hearts and pull
them out: then we shall have another war.
But here the companies' rushing, muttering growls
have scattered like swallows into the air;
the streams of billowing smoke have long ago
gone to ground, and the pathos of their cheers
has settled into military rows.
The brave have made into a kind of grace
the sheer forgetful splendor of this place.

McPherson's Barn

How long, O Lord, will the old work go on?
The calves stamp still, the green fields are still mad;
the brown blood on the hard mud won't fade
and the soldiers' ghosts will never be gone.
In summer the sun off the boards is blinding;
we tramp the paths to the hot stalls, eyes closed,
sweat soaking and sticking to our smelly clothes;
the flies whine all the time while we're aligning
our balky beasts for milking. In winter
all we do is mend and mend and mend
what's torn or worn by daily use: splintered
pails, warped boards, frayed reins, snapped bits — in the long
cold hours at night — moaning owl hours without end —
thinking, reliving, mending what went wrong.

WILLOUGHBY RUN

Time is a moral conjunction as real as a dream,
a murderous burbling image that feels like a stream;
needful and lethal, divine as ephemeral day,
it comes out of nowhere and goes on its voracious way;
a drug drunk at sunrise, necessity sweet and unyielding,
it plays in our veins and etches our brains, making real
what was only a syllabic fall from the clouds of the gods:
their will and our wills wrestling down the rough run of our fates.

So this morning we came and we waded the reflecting odds
and attacked. There is never a time when it isn't too late.
The dead knelt and bled while the victors victoriously won;
the shot stopped and dreamed while the water made fast what was done.
I looked over Jordan, and what did I see —
the stumbling angels abandoning me.

23RD PSALM

1.

A meadow is a morning to be tasted,
cool dew and overripe rain teeth to tongue;
nothing that is perfect can be wasted.

In God's bosom I shall not feel hunger.
I am a lamb; He carries me in arms
to the tenderest shoots and the small grass;

He lifts my head to the milk in His palm.
The sun goes slowly toward the waiting west
and rises to the distant bell of noon.

There is no breeze, and the heat sinks in deep;
by afternoon the tender lamb is grown.
Now ravens stir from their heroic sleep,

and gray wolves, pagan since the world was ice,
smell the warm, sullen blood of sacrifice.

2.

Where I lie down, the summer's running pasture
will grow over me, the yellow flowers
and the spreading clover will be gathered
together by the same earnest hours
that round the days toward August and September
(the waves of footsteps, murmurings and cries;
the agonies that no-one will remember);
the shadows that lope on where someone dies
will drag the harvest after them in fires;
the loft in the dark barn will be full to the rafters,
bales of crackling hay thrown higher, and still higher,
toward dull November skies forever after
the waves of footsteps, murmurings and cries,
the agonies that no-one will remember.

3.

He leadeth me beside still waters.
That afternoon, the Wheatfield's parched soil
could not assume the runny parts of slaughter,
could not resolve the slipperiness of toil;
but runnelled off in rivulets like veins,
the blood of many sacrificial lambs
cut criss-cross on a twilit page of stains
and mingled with the curses of the damned.
He leadeth me beside still waters
where soldiers dropped their roaring, weary heads
exchanging lifeblood for the local water,
and swimming in the Ganges of the dead.
He leadeth me, He leadeth me;
with His own hand He leadeth me.

4.

Again, again, though the golden bowl be broken
and the silver cord severed, the past trail
into the sky, the womb's light is spoken
and we are born into a world that dies.
Again from the meadow, and up from the palm-like pond,
the desiccated souls are gathered up,
the un-named souls are claimed, the names put on,
mirage of time poured back into the cup.
Our broken bones are gathered in the dust,
last exhalations drawn into the flower,
condemned and sentenced never to be lost —
such is mercy's carefulness and power.
The soldier's pallid cheek may not stay pale;
the tire and tear of mercy does not fail.

5.

"I walk the valley of death; I fear no evil."
But who can say the shadow, and the black wing
above it that comes and goes as it wills,
do not make us kneel beneath the sting
of chance? — and if we walk at all, we creep
like beetles, hoping to go unnoticed.
That cosy hope is evidence of sleep:
will God relent if we surrender first?
Who is this who walks without that fear?
He has passed the last stand of bravery,
has felt the step of another one near
more casual and purposeful than fate;
he is happy, he is filled with grace:
he has finally come to know his place.

6.

They followed him like sheep; they felt comfort
in orders, from doomed juniors took solace.
The torn up corps, Sickles' Union Third, fought
where a line of statues grounded solid
founders now on a horizon of grass.
His steady rank and file fell well here then,
declining ripe alfalfa as they passed,
his disobedience felt by his men.
Where is the solace of a childhood Lord
who loves us and protects us from all ill
and puts the heathen to the righteous sword —
is he who cradles also he who kills?
Whose are the rod and staff that comfort me —
what is a god that none but the dead see?

7.

The presence of my enemies brings solace —
the press and rush of infantry, the firm
defense, the close danger from which no space
falls away on any side, the full warm
hurrahs or yells. How could the first man live
alone? — that open, silent sky above,
with no brutal refusals, no relief
from possibles, nothing cruel to make love
a presence breathing, hungering, grasping
against him in the night: who would not sin
to make an enemy even of God? —
make him wrathfully refuse to let you in
to that infinite open bed and board,
and face you daily with a flaming sword.

8.

If when the pain is over He anoints
my head and fills my cup, I shall look back.
The valley of the shadow shall lie quiet:
empty corpses open-mouthed, black
and swollen in the sun, etched in long grass;
small, rusty trickles in the trampled dirt —
blown debris where the droning armies passed —
a paper collar from a colonel's shirt —
just once, look back, for high above we hear
an angel singing in the noisy blue
while streams of soldiers, resurrected, bear
praises, thanksgivings, ascending to
forgetful rooms and halls of never, never —
to dwell in the House of the Lord forever.

A Chapel on a Hill

On Seminary Ridge a chapel waits
for casualties of internecine wars.
Attentive in its pews, the patient Fates
are seated with their backs to open doors.
Come in. The airy windows spread soft light
on saints and judges, angels, multitudes
who left their homes and flocked here for a fight.
The organ studies endless interludes,
the chaplain pages many fine translations;
the people faint for presence of the Lord.
Long waiting is the final tribulation.
Outside, the last apostles spread the word
and hope to be among the ones impressed
to carry in the bleeding, dying guests.

Admiringly, a steeple pries the sky,
a lever of pure white, high as the eye
can try. A solid block of bricks supports
the carpentry that elegantly courts
the Courts of Praise. But it is no use.
Sometimes it all feels prosaically flat:
sawdust and masonry, nails, tacks, paint,
a little of this and a little of that
trying to make something of something that aint.
And other times, let's say usually,
the picture of it all exhausts the mind
with suggestions: the Sea of Galilee,
the startled laughter of a man born blind,
a little box of straw in Bethlehem,
the glimmer of a new Jerusalem.

THE SILVER CORD

The soldier's body is a silver cord
suspended on a peremptory line
taut and singing like a poet's rhyme,
unraveling from a tutelary lord —
inventor of the algebra of chance —
who wanders purposefully by the hour
through carnage, suffering, and flowers
looking for the perfect circumstance.

See now, he stoops, this peregrine of love,
tracing a hunter with his flight, arranging
random stars so that they seem to prove
the universe is really not so strange,
traveling the firmament above,
that fragrant field still blooming disarranged.

The born are mustered into glorious wars —
ah, singers, that agree to sing no more.

A RESTING PLACE

Green goes quickly to the memory,
the red of barns, the dipping curve of fields
lying like a soft hand upon the soul;
the light itself some mornings seems so old
that, interspersed among the patient summer trees,
you almost sense the soldiers murmuring —
sitting in their numbers, measuring
a day that has been halted and prolonged.

Then we rush on, become the traffic
down that empty road — gin the noise, the fumes,
and the money: it is only for the pay
that Time has enlisted. Poor Eternity
lounges, smokes a cigarette, flicks
the ashes on this old, familiar tomb.

THREE

Three soldiers folded into shallow graves
beneath the deep, deep green of summer grass:
One, a Massachusetts man in blue,
an unsung hero; loyal, brave, and true.

Two, a mumbling Galilean veteran
prone to prayer but willing to pitch in
when all else fails, a volunteer. He died
in the sun while trying to read the sky.

Third, a relatively new recruit,
a brooding boy, knapsack heavy with home —
dealing out his last precious tin of fruit,
ripped open by a shell; here are his bones.

Invisible and mythical as ghosts,
legendary. Without them we are lost.

UNKNOWN

They are the early ones, the skirmishers,
those who unfurl their faces to the wind,
those who walk to where there are no shadows.
The white wind of tomorrow snows their bones
out into a wide field of memory
whose space, infinite space, melts them with its
distances. They, our brothers gone before,
walk through the call of Father Abraham.

We are their shadows marching to the fight.
We come, a hundred hundred thousand more.
One by one, file by file and rank on rank,
named with names like wheel tracks in dewy grass —
with names like horses' prints in flattened grass —
we follow them, we follow them, follow.

STEVENS' KNOLL

The earth is fair, and memories are phrased
for dreaming it. One spring or summer long
ago, when heavy warmth spread on the grass
like candlelight, and consciousness could end
in leaves or the calm temper of the sky,
we rested here together, you and I:
we traced the same horizon I do now
until our hands, as light as wings, folded
beatitudes of scarlet-shafted clouds,
and the river of their war ran cold,
though they fought through afternoons of red
hammering for union and liberty,
volunteering generations of dead
in the plunging hearts of artillery.

STONE SOLDIER

A hardened veteran aims with hammer cocked
behind a two-low row of stones. His eyes
are tired but determined; they are locked
toward that distant enemy, tightened
like his hands, his jaw, his stone clothes, his skin,
the heart within him. A spray of cold gray
fern once fanned back against his angled shin,
now crystallized like veins in ice. They say
the universe was made from thought one day.
What was this highly detailed thinker thinking?
What was so firm within his beating brain,
that turned him stiff beyond imagining?
Our pleasure is to guess it if we can.
In 1863 he was a man.

BATTLEFIELD

The statuary on the battlefield
is registered in heaven. We made an oath:
"preserve, protect, defend" — so registered
as well. It is convenient that both
responsibilities increase with age,
so that when Fortune's wheel comes round again
we will be hot with appropriate rage
and the willingness to furnish men:

their metal attitudes at the ready—
swords and carbines for the cavalry;
waiting thunder for artillery;
the tensely lounging, patient infantry --
vigilant among the tourist crowds
and transitory battlements of clouds.

Such is our bond, our care, our old office
discharged in season and out of season,
enrolling us in solemn, marching hosts
more immutable than rhyme or reason.

. . . thin trees reach for full leaf, wind is soughing,
patches of light swatch the ground, long ago,
long ago.

. . . Where else can we go?

SEPTEMBER

A path along an ancient wall, dry ground
worn by walkers passing in twos and threes,
beginning to be overgrown with weeds —
an old farm lane is used for musing now.
And many years before the battle passed
across the crest and down this rocky hill,
you would have touched a narrow hunters' trail
if you had crouched and felt the parted grass.
And long, long years before a history
was traced in brains that marked the moons with stones,
this granite rose and wrestled, cracked and groaned
from floors of ten successive, endless seas,
where we recount our childhoods and our wars
beneath a universe of flaming stars.

WOMAN IN WHITE

In the woods of Culp's Hill at Gettysburg, they say,
a beautiful woman comes gliding at night,
silent as stone and knowing her way,
she appears in a garment of radiant white.
Beside Spangler's Spring they have seen her sometimes,
or up on the hill through the shadowy trees:
she walks in the moonlight along the old lines
where soldiers still suffer but nobody sees.
She mourns for her lover who died in the battle
and looks for him, grieving, long nights on Culp's Hill.
If lost there alone you once hear a death rattle
and feel in your bones the long moan of a chill,
fold your hands on your heart and say a goodnight
to your faithful, your true love, your lady in white!

LIBERTY TURNS AWAY

She turns, turns and looks into a cloudy,
dimmed sun, casually gripping her laurel
like a lariat. She's a little frowzy
and with sleeve uprolled looks somewhat disheveled.
Is she bored with us at last, we who lived
with her these long domestic years, married
we thought? By and by we treated her like
a wife, then a cook, a servant, and tried
to buy her enough to keep her at home
while we went out — mostly out of habit,
because while it was nice to have her at home
it must be admitted, we took her for granted.
Come, give us again those hot looks, do —
when you are cold, there's none more terrible than you.

SENTRIES

While they watch, the wild azalea grows,
wisteria lengthens; artillery lunettes
are overcrept by locust. They stare through lost sleep
an icy century—wild sentries
in frozen frenzy, fearless Icelanders,
hard-helmeted, stone-sworded,
cooly careless Vikings lounging
in lonely spring's lush Valhalla.

The gray wave has wavered away—
the cold wail, the killing fox-call,
Confederate scream: sullen and silent
in simple graves, gregarious as grain,
ghosts in longships, leaning lengthwise
green-eyed, some summer rising again.

He is the color
of trees, a trunk struck early, shed already,
an adjutant of winter waiting still
and confident amid this loud glory.

ECONOMY

The wounded and the strange, the bright faces
pooling sun in summer bundled off, mown;
the living, sweeping time before them, hasty
always to be gone away and grown;
the earth, a bit of stardust with its fjords
and mountains, meadowlands, and seething fields;
the heavens with their undiscovered lords;
all time and space: everything must yield —
whatever is, becoming never more;
whatever has a name becoming words
assumed into the alabaster wind
of procreation willing without end:
whatever has been thought or said again
drawn up into the sower's hand.

BROUGHT FORTH

Those men were smaller then, and younger too:
they were young enough to be our sons.
They were too gay and brave and innocent
to handle heavy guns.
They wept too easily, sentimental
as could be, those tender-hearted sons
of liberty; and to defend their mothers
were quick to shoulder guns.
They sang while marching, sang while in their camps,
our happy children, our good, kind, gentle sons
who never should have known the steel of war,
the hot, dry smoke of guns —
but when we cried in time's wide womb for fathers
answered, We are the ones, We are the ones.

LEAVES ON STONES

A soldiers' cemetery in the fall
seems beautiful to us, pure poetry:
white, numbered marble stones that might appall
appear universal when orderly
and garlanded with bright colors dying;
they make us muse on immortality.
Days are lines, poems, falling into time,
and in the memory appear to rhyme.

War and poetry stay when God blows away:
pathology that feels like salvation,
the beautiful necessity to pay
all for nothing, holy superstition,
the rosy glory in these soldiers' bones,
soiled gestures of the fallen and unknown.

. . . let the damned pretend like heroes,
let the sinners save the human race. . .

Here the soldiers lie, released from names,
garlanded with leaves these serene days,
forgotten everywhere but in this place,
invisible as God's saluted face.

Like an old blood sample, yellowed with age,
the sunset in a photographer's lens . . .

CONTINGENCY

All's bloody round the sun; a hand drips down

from up above somewhere: does the pale star

wait keen and cool across a still high noon

for this tense gunslinger, and will he hear

the small word "draw" before it gets the drop

on him? Or is the ball a soul in white,

solemnly dropped into its fresh clay cup,

rolled down from a dread hand and a dread height?

Is the morning fire arising

From a dewy dust,

And the heavy fingers bending

From an iron rest:

Mars or Christ as bleeding sun ascending? —

and we to sleep the sleep of damned or just?

ON THE ROSE FARM

Who is that singing in the sloping field
beyond the Peach Orchard, on Rose's place?
We once saw Indians a-running there,
not seeing us — fleeting, light, a foot-race
with some dark future baying at their heels —
us, perhaps; that time we were the ones aware.
But the singing? Pre-occupied and light,
repetitious, high — a swallow's flight —
like a young wife setting out her wash
after a staring, trembling, earthly night,
the young father flown to memory
unaware like a flitting, buckskinned dash
right out from smoking lines of infantry;
then ceased, and gone. Then the silence!

The soldier in his shabby battle line
walks forward through an ancient discipline,
accepts the arbitrary ordered lines,
believes the purifying force of rhyme.

MYSTERIES

Like rows of snow the harvest will go white:
the sun's exhuming roar has raised the seed
up from its wormy, clinging winter bed.
The dying poet cries, "More light! More light!"

Streams of green in the fields march over dry
swaths cut and desiccated in the sun,
a corps of roaring order, stalks and blades like guns
and bayonets crowding toward a blue sky;
the dead brown and bundled into stiff bales
and the sun-struck living already pale.

The poet slips from poetry and dies,
a seedy blanket straightened on his breast
over old hands folded on the gray chest,
and warm gold disks placed on his upturned eyes.

It is cold and quiet out here
with two dead armies deep and near.
Where are the cannoneers, the officers
with eyes fixed in distance-sharpened gazes,
the slouched horsemen, the jumpy couriers?
The boys with home and hate smoothed from their faces
believe no more. We are their file-closers.

REVERSES

The swatch of leaves, November brown, lightly
spread by a ghostly old oak, betrays no
picket's watch, embarrasses no stealthy
tread, is no efficient cause of death.
The only watchers now are cannons, iron
twelve-pounder Parrots, reinforced breeches —
alone, these two, a section, short four —
shelved on this battlefield museum.

Meanwhile the rest of the battery fought
a lost fight with age, limbered to the wheel
of time, dully surprised by skirmishers
of rust, transmigrating to railroad tracks,
aching bridges, surrendered to disuse,
flaking into brittle leaves like verse.

. . . musket barrels clack again
atop a long, high row of stone — the clank
and crush of infantry who crowd in and bend
to aim and fire, rank kneeling behind rank.
Beneath this lingering filagree of leaves they thank
God for a gate; they pass through and ascend.

SNOW ON THE CELTIC CROSS

The Irish Brigade left a monument
at Gettysburg: a Celtic cross in bronze
with numbers of the New York regiments
in line beneath a shamrock embossed.
At the base an Irish Wolfhound lies,
its large face pressed upon the ground, an image
of loss, reminder that all loveliness dies,
and grief is the one sure consequence of rage.
Today the sky is gray, and salty snow
has settled sparingly from very high
upon the beast, upon the cross, down
upon the fallen autumn leaves. He cries,
God, for the Irish, to be sure, and for
everything made beautiful by war.

First Snow

... a blurry sun shines
like a hole — has never looked so all alone,
has never seen the earth so flat and wide,
laid hope aside, has never dipped so low
and still melts no snow; is tired. ...
Sometimes I feel like a motherless child,
sometimes I feel like a motherless child,
a long way from home.

VIOLENCE

Torn clouds are residues of cosmic flame,
sudden eruptions bleeding spumes of dust
shot through with violet, extruding blues
charged end to end with filaments of white,
sweeping across time, billowing in gusts
the size of galaxies, no two the same:
the first bright light still multiplies and spews
new fires of violence across old night.

The laws in nebulae and seas and souls,
if laws there be, must play the same for all,
or else we would be innocent, not lost,
alien on the very grass of home,
no flesh and blood to pay the total cost
of spoken love, immortal and alone.

DECEMBER

He —whom prophets say this month is born—
in a stubble field of straw, a stretch of stalks
adjacent to a swath of rickety corn
swept away in a hot, dry August, walks
somewhere toward the dying of the day
and listens as the distant church-bells chime.
He's thinking of a manger full of hay,
where, swaddled in the circling bands of time,
he cries not for the world, but at the light.
He disappears into the winter night.
See where the harrowed steps turned under,
following the sinking autumn rain;
fence rails lie where hurried hands of summer
left them; the snow is on the grass again.

YEAR'S END

. . . Where fresh cannons lunged in high noonday heat,
now relics rest in stubble, dashed of breath,
standing as the dead stand on their feet,
no limbering, slugged still as stone to earth.
A statue holds a dark arm pointing: there
the enemy came charging up the hill,
where now a perturbation of the air
would only raise a soundless, solemn chill.
Time lifts its light fingers to the blinds
in this quiet museum of the mind.

THE END OF THE WORLD

The Lord looked down from heaven on the sons
of men, and lo, the sons had turned to stone.
"What shall I do with my hard-hearted ones? —
For it is not fit that I live alone."
But all creation silent lay, and still.
The hawk had ceased to tumble on the air;
the badger wandered no more on her hill —
instead, a soldier lay and moldered there
and sweeping scavengers revolved in moody
circles in the sky. "I shall descend," God
said, "and look for my beloved Son, Christ."
But Christ had fallen in with mortal men
God wandered in the world's weeds and was lost.
The Holy Ghost put down the empty pen.

OLD LIGHT

A deeper blue assumes the sky tonight
than any we have ever seen. Yet snow falls.
Down through dark clouds comes such an elder light
that were it concentrated to a star
would drive wise men mad, and appall
God's child. For it is so unearthly far
in coming that everything it touches
with its spoken and re-echoed fire
should tremble like the backs of burning birches:
paper twisting into ashes up the skies.
This snow is rising; the earth is on fire
in the cold: there will be no Bethlehem
left, no straw unburnt to cradle in,
no air to lift or hear an angel choir.

MIDNIGHT

Sweet Eden was a battlefield, its night
sky flowery with clouds and poison moon,
brave darkness lush with incandescent air
murmuring like a voice of someone there —
a military park today, the fight
revisited by folks from everywhere
romantic as a solitary loon.

So you are mortal too? — a malady
diurnal, for in dreams the soul is fed
with heavenly food in serried ranks of endless day
where rank on rank pale angels veil their faces
as the endless casualties are read:
the distant eyes of mortals newly thronging —
their staggering forgetfulness, their longing.

KENT GRAMM

Kent Gramm is the author of *Gettysburg: A Meditation on War and Values*, *November: Lincoln's Elegy at Gettysburg*, *Somebody's Darling: Essays on the Civil War*, and the novel, *Clare*. He is a winner of the Hart Crane Memorial Poetry Prize. Currently a Professor of English at Wheaton College in Illinois, he has taught writing and American Studies at several institutions in Germany and the United States and is Program Director of the Seminary Ridge Historic Preservation Foundation in Gettysburg. A native of Wisconsin, where he now resides, Kent Gramm was educated at Carroll College, Princeton Theological Seminary, the University of Tuebingen, and the University of Wisconsin-Milwaukee.

CHRIS E. HEISEY

National Merit Award-Winning Photographer

The evocative Civil War imagery of Chris Heisey has graced the pages of more than 70 worldwide publications, including *National Geographic Traveler*, *Popular Photography*, and *North & South*. He began photographing battlefields in 1990, drawing inspiration from the acclaimed Ken Burns PBS series entitled *The Civil War*. Commissioned by the National Park Service and the U.S. Congress for numerous assignments, his work has earned several merit citations, including a recent Photo of the Century award.

He's a native Pennsylvanian growing up in a small town less than an hour from Gettysburg—a hallowed battlefield that he has visited more than 1,200 times dating from 1972. Along with his wife, Kim, and son, Aaron, he lives near Harrisburg, where he works as a photojournalist for *The Catholic Witness*, published by the Diocese of Harrisburg.

INDEX OF IMAGES

By Chris E. Heisey

Gettysburg National Military Park is home to the world's largest outdoor sculpture display, where more than 1,400 monuments and memorials dot the immortal landscape. Each monument has a story to tell us, each is a moment of sacrifice that is forever frozen in time. The photographer honors all of the soldiers who were lost at Gettysburg and acknowledges all of the artists over the years that have gone before to this hallowed field of memory.

SOURCES

Brown, Herbert O. and Nitz, Dwight V. *Fields of Glory: The Facts Book of the Battle of Gettysburg.* Gettysburg, PA: Thomas Publications, 1996.

Coddington, Edwin B. *The Gettysburg Campaign: A Study in Command.* Carmichael, CA: Touchstone Books, 1983.

Dowdy, Clifford and Manarin, Louis (eds). *The Wartime Papers of R. E. Lee.* New York: Bramhall House, 1961.

Freeman, Douglas Southall. *Lee's Lieutenants: A Study in Command.* New York: Scribner, 1997.

Garrison, Webb. *Brady's Civil War.* Guilford, CT: Lyons Press, September 2000.

Hawthorne, Frederick. *Gettysburg: Stories of Men and Monuments.* Association of Licensed Battlefield Guides, 1988

Pfanz, Harry W. *Gettysburg: The Second Day.* Chapel Hill, NC: University of North Carolina Press, 1987.